EXTRAORDINARY WOMEN

Michelle OBAMA

Robin Doak

Chicago, Illinois

To contact Capstone Global Library please
phone 800-747-4992, or visit our website
www.capstonepub.com

Edited by Abby Colich
Designed by Philippa Jenkins
Picture research by Ruth Blair
Production by Helen McCreath
Originated by Capstone Global Library
Printed and bound in China by Leo Paper
Group

17 16 15 14 13
10 9 8 7 6 5 4 3 2 1

**Library of Congress Cataloging-in-
Publication Data**
Doak, Robin S. (Robin Santos), 1963-
 Michelle Obama / Robin Doak.
  pages cm.—(Extraordinary women)
 Includes bibliographical references and
index.
 ISBN 978-1-4109-5940-9 (hb)—ISBN 978-
1-4109-5948-5 (pb) 1. Obama, Michelle,
1964—Juvenile literature. 2. Presidents'
spouses—United States—Biography—Juvenile literature. 3. Legislators' spouses—United States—Biography—Juvenile literature. 4.
African American women lawyers—Illinois—
Chicago—Biography—Juvenile literature. 5.
African American women—Biography—Juvenile literature. 6. Chicago (Ill.)—Biography—Juvenile literature. I. Title.
 E909.O24D63 2014
 973.932092—dc23   2013017126
 [B]

Acknowledgments
The author and publisher are grateful to
the following for permission to reproduce
copyright material: Alamy: p. 11 (© Travel
Division Images); Corbis: pp. 6 (© Joseph
Sohm/Visions of America), 7 (© Rick
Friedman), 8 (© Brian Murphy/Icon SMI),
9 (© Splash News/Splash News), 12 (© Joe
Wrinn/Harvard University/Handout), 16 (©
Obama For America/Handout /Reuters), 23
(© Jason Reed/Reutersz), 27 (© Bettmann),
33 (© Callie Shell/Obama Transition Office/
Handout /Reuters), 35 (© Chuck Kennedy/
The White House), 39 (© Daniel Hambury/
Reuters); Getty Images: pp. 5 (Alex Wong),
19 (Alex Wong), 20 (Scott Olson), 24 (Tasos
Katopodis), 25 (Mario Tama), 26 (MANDEL
NGAN/AFP), 28 (Scott Olson), 30 (Joe
Raedle), 31 (Chip Somodevilla), 34 (Win
McNamee), 37 (RDA/Hulton Archive), 40
(Alex Wong), 41 (JEWEL SAMAD/AFP), 42
(MANDEL NGAN/AFP);
Library of Congress: p. 21; Official White
House Photo: pp. 14 (Pete Souza), 15 (Pete
Souza), 29 (Pete Souza), 32 (Pete Souza),
38 (Pete Souza); PA Photos: p. 22 (FRANK
POLICH/AP); Rex Features: pp. 17 (INS
News Agency Ltd), 18 (Sipa Press), 36;
Shutterstock: pp. 10 (© gary718).

Cover photograph of Michelle Obama
reproduced with permission from Getty
Images (Mark Wilson).

CONTENTS

Making History

On January 20, 2009, more than a million people gathered on the National Mall in Washington, D.C., to watch history in the making. Around the world, millions more watched by television or on the Internet as Barack Obama was sworn in as the first African-American president. Standing next to him was his best friend and strongest supporter, his wife Michelle Obama.

Nearly four years later, after being elected for a second term as president, Barack told Americans, "I wouldn't be the man I am today without the woman who agreed to marry me 20 years ago." He has called Michelle "the boss" and "his rock." So who is Michelle Obama?

Michelle held Abraham Lincoln's Bible as her husband became the first African-American president of the United States.

A huge crowd assembled to watch Barack Obama become president on January 20, 2009.

Who Is Michelle Obama?

Born Michelle Robinson in Chicago, Illinois, she was a beloved daughter and a talented and determined student. Later she became a hard-working lawyer and an advocate for social justice. After meeting Barack, she became a community organizer, a wife, and mom.

Michelle Obama's role as first lady has made her famous around the world. Calm, intelligent, and caring, she is one of the most popular first ladies ever. She has used her position and popularity to do good by speaking out for military families, children, and women around the world.

BREAKING BOUNDARIES

HEIGHT

At 5'11" Michelle ties Eleanor Roosevelt as the tallest first lady. In fact, she is the same height as three former presidents (Grover Cleveland, Woodrow Wilson, and Herbert Hoover) and taller than 18 past presidents.

Michelle Robinson

The first lady's story begins in Chicago, Illinois. On January 17, 1964, Michelle LaVaughn Robinson was born in a city hospital. Michelle's parents, Marian and Fraser Robinson, were lifelong Chicago residents. Marian was a homemaker. Fraser worked at the city's water department.

Brother Craig

Michelle was the Robinsons' second child. Her brother Craig was a year and a half old when she was born. Growing up, Michelle idolized her big brother. The two slept in the living room of the family's small house on Chicago's South Shore. The sleeping area was separated from the rest of the living room by a partition. Late at night, they would talk to each other before falling asleep.

Michelle grew up in Chicago with her parents and older brother Craig.

Craig introduced his sister to the nation at the 2008 Democratic National Convention.

Michelle's Parents

Marian and Fraser expected their children to work hard, play hard, and succeed. Even before Craig and Michelle started school, their mother had taught them to read. Marian also taught her children to speak their minds and pursue their dreams. "Don't let people stop you," she told her kids.

Fraser was a role model for his children too. Even though he suffered from a debilitating disease called multiple sclerosis (MS), Fraser worked hard all his life. He taught Craig and Michelle integrity, responsibility, and hard work.

THEN and NOW

Slave Ancestors

In 2009 a researcher traced one of Michelle Obama's ancestors back to a South Carolina plantation in 1850. That year a six-year-old slave girl named Melvinia was mentioned in a slave owner's will. The will valued Melvinia, who would later become Michelle's great-great-great grandmother, at $475. Michelle's family tree also includes white and Indian ancestors.

Michelle's brother, Craig, also found much success as an adult. After a career in finance, he became head men's baskeball coach at Oregon State University.

An Outstanding Student

As a young child, Michelle was naturally smart. But Marian and Fraser Robinson made sure that both Michelle and her brother learned to work hard and be disciplined. The Robinsons assigned both kids chores around the house. Craig and Michelle washed the dishes during the week. Michelle cleaned the bathroom on Saturdays.

Michelle's earliest teachers recognized her talents and drive. Like her brother Craig, Michelle was allowed to skip the second grade. In middle school, she was chosen to participate in a program for talented students. As part of the program, she took advanced science and French classes at a local college.

High School Days

In 1977 Michelle was chosen to attend a special high school. Whitney Young High School is an elite school that accepts only the most outstanding students. The school provides challenging and advanced classes that prepare students to attend college and be leaders.

Each day, Michelle traveled three hours roundtrip to and from Whitney Young High School. Michelle enjoyed high school and was well liked by her teachers and fellow students. She was a member of the National Honor Society and also served in student government.

A Natural Leader

Michelle's family saw her promise early on. Marian Robinson said,

> "She wanted to do the right thing all the time without being told, and she wanted to be the best at things. She liked winning."

Brother Craig called her the natural leader of the neighborhood kids.

Michelle with her high school prom date in 1982.

Branching Out

As an African-American child growing up in Chicago, Michelle witnessed prejudice and discrimination aimed at African Americans. Her parents told her that one way to overcome prejudice was through education. After graduating from high school, Michelle followed her brother Craig to Princeton University in New Jersey. Marian Robinson took a job as a secretary to help her kids pay the high tuition.

Presidents James Madison and Woodrow Wilson also graduated from Princeton, as well as U.S. Supreme Court Justices Samuel Alito, Elena Kagan, and Sonia Sotomayor.

College Days

At Princeton, Michelle stood out as one of the best and brightest students. She majored in sociology, the study of how societies work. She also took courses in African-American studies. During her time at Princeton, Michelle was active in the college community. She volunteered with the Third World Center, a group that helped minority students by providing day care, tutoring, and other services.

THEN and NOW

Charlotte E. Ray, Lawyer

In February 1872, 22-year-old Charlotte E. Ray graduated from Howard Law School, becoming the first black female lawyer in the United States. That same year, she became the first woman allowed to try cases in front of the U.S. Supreme Court. She suffered from prejudice and discrimination throughout her life and career. Ray died in 1911.

Howard University was started for African Americans in 1867.

After graduating from Princeton with honors in 1985, Michelle set her sights on becoming a lawyer. She was accepted at Harvard Law School, one of the top law schools in the nation. When she graduated in 1988, she decided to return to Chicago and start her law career close to her family.

Fact
Michelle Obama is the third first lady with a postgraduate degree.

Meeting Barack Obama

Soon after graduating from Harvard, Michelle was offered a job at Sidley and Austin, a corporate law firm in Chicago. At the firm, Michelle helped large companies protect the rights to their products and ideas.

An Instant Attraction

In the summer of 1989, a young law student named Barack Obama began a summer internship at the law firm. Michelle was assigned to be his mentor, or guide. The outspoken, confident Barack was immediately fascinated by his intelligent coworker with the warm laugh. Using his well-known charm and sense of humor, he tried to talk Michelle into dating him.

Fact
Michelle is the third first lady born in Chicago.

Barack Obama was a law student when he met Michelle in Chicago.

Engagement
Former Site of Gordon's
500 N. Clark Street

Sidley & Austin
Chase Tower
10 S. Dearborn Street

Kenwood Neighborhood
5046 S. Greenwood

First Kiss Plaque
1400 E. 53rd Street

First Home Together
5450 S. East View Park

Childhood Home
7436 S. Euclid Avenue

Wedding
Trinity Church
532 W. 95th Street

This map marks important places in Chicago in Michelle's life and the Obamas' relationship.

First Date

Eventually, Michelle gave in. On the couple's first date, they went to an art museum, had lunch, and saw a movie. The Robinsons didn't think the relationship would last long. Michelle had high standards, and few men could measure up. After a month, Michelle put Barack to an important test: she had him play basketball with her brother. After the game, Craig reported that Barack was a good guy.

Just Friends

Barack and Michelle had different views of where their relationship should go. Barack thought,

"I'm going to work my magic on her."

Michelle thought,

"This guy is going to be a good friend of mine."

She warned Barack that she had no time for dating.

Changing Paths

After Barack's summer internship ended, he returned to Harvard Law School to finish his law degree. But he and Michelle carried on a long-distance relationship. When he returned to Chicago after graduating, the two continued their romance.

In the early 1990s, Michelle began rethinking her path in life. In 1990 her best friend died of cancer. In March 1991 her father died. The deaths of these two important people made Michelle think seriously about what she wanted to do with her future. Michelle was not happy practicing corporate law. She wanted to find a job that would allow her to help those who were less fortunate.

In 1991 Michelle took a job working for Chicago Mayor Richard M. Daley.

Valerie Jarrett, a close friend of Michelle's, was chosen as President Obama's senior adviser in 2008.

Serving the Community

In 1991 Michelle began work as an assistant to Chicago Mayor Richard M. Daley. Later, she worked as a commissioner for the city's planning and development department. During this time of change, one thing remained constant: her growing admiration and love for Barack. The two shared a deep desire to improve Chicago communities, help those in need, and make a difference in the world.

Valerie Jarrett

Valerie Jarrett started as Michelle's boss at Chicago City Hall, but she became a close friend of both Michelle and Barack. Jarrett talked about her earliest opinions of the pair. She said,

"Their life experiences were different, but yet they had the same core values, the same sense...that to those who much is given, much is expected."

The happy couple posed together on their wedding day.

Making a Commitment

After a couple years of dating Barack, Michelle was ready to make a more serious commitment. But Barack told her that he didn't believe in marriage. The topic became a sore subject between the two. However, one night at dinner Michelle found a small box on her dessert plate. Inside was an engagement ring.

Barack and Michelle were married in Chicago on October 3, 1992. After their honeymoon in California, they soon moved into their own apartment in Hyde Park, a neighborhood on the South Side of Chicago.

Working with Students

The coming year brought more change for Michelle. In 1993 she took a job as the director for a nonprofit group called Public Allies. Public Allies, which Barack helped found, prepares young people to participate in public service projects. In her new role, Michelle found college students and others to work in homeless shelters and city offices.

Barack was busy too. He was becoming well-known around Chicago as a hard-working and intelligent community advocate. He was active in the city's Democratic Party, and he would soon decide to devote all of his energies to politics.

Best Friends

After they married, Michelle said,

> "Barack didn't pledge riches, only a life that would be interesting. On that promise he delivered."

Twenty years later, Barack still calls Michelle the love of his life and his best friend.

Barack and his half-brother Abongo on his wedding day to Michelle in 1992.

Family and Fame

The year 1996 was one of major change in the Obama household. That year, Michelle took on a new career challenge at the University of Chicago. She began work as the college's first Associate Dean of Student Services. Her new job centered on recruiting and training students from the university to volunteer in nearby neighborhoods.

Barack Enters Politics

In 1996 Barack was elected to his first term as an Illinois state senator. Michelle had not been happy when her husband wanted to run for office. Barack was already busy. He had just finished writing his first book, and he held an important job as a law professor at the University of Chicago.

Barack and Michelle both held jobs at the University of Chicago Law School.

Michelle has always supported Barack's political career. She attended his swearing in ceremony to the U.S. Senate in 2005 with their daughters.

Michelle also knew that holding elected office was one of Barack's dreams. So she gave him all of her support. Michelle became his hardest-working and most valuable campaign volunteer. She knocked on doors to gather signatures so Barack's name could appear on the ballot. She organized other volunteers. She was also an asset in another important way. While Barack could sometimes seem stiff and distant, Michelle's warmth and friendliness won voters' hearts.

BREAKING BOUNDARIES

COMMUNITY SERVICE CENTER

In 1997 Michelle developed the first community service program at the University of Chicago. She modeled the program after Public Allies, where she had worked until 1996. Her Community Service Center (CSC) still exists today. The CSC has offered thousands of students the chance to volunteer with Chicago community organizations.

Balancing Family and Career

In 1998 the Obamas welcomed their first child, a daughter they named Malia Ann. Malia, born on the Fourth of July, was named after Barack's mother, Stanley Ann Dunham. Ann had died in 1995 from cancer.

Malia's birth was the beginning of a new focus for Michelle. To spend more time with her baby, Michelle went from full time to part time at the University of Chicago. The state government was in recess for the summer, so Senator Obama was home from Springfield. The family had three months to be together.

Sasha and Malia Obama with their parents in 2004.

THEN and NOW

Mary Todd Lincoln

Barack Obama is often compared to Abraham Lincoln. So how does Michelle stack up against Mary Todd Lincoln, the 17th first lady? Although Mary was born in Kentucky, she later called Chicago her home. And like Michelle, Mary raised two of her three children in the White House.

Mary Todd and Abraham
Lincoln with their three sons

Back to Work

In October Michelle returned to work and Barack went back to Springfield. With her husband gone for most of the week, Michelle often found herself taking care of Malia alone. When the babysitter couldn't make it, Michelle was the one who missed work days and canceled meetings. As Barack's political career grew, the Obamas settled into the pattern of him as a "weekend dad." This was sometimes difficult for the family.

21

A Growing Family

In 2000 Barack set his sights on Washington, D.C. That year, he ran unsuccessfully for election to the U.S. Congress. Barack admitted that his wife was "not wild" about the campaign. Although Michelle helped as much as possible, Malia was her top priority. With Barack away from Chicago even more than usual, Michelle made sure life at home was normal for her daughter.

The year after Barack's failed election, Michelle and Barack welcomed their second child, Natasha. Known as Sasha, the newest Obama was born on June 10. From this time on, Michelle described herself as "first and foremost…Malia and Sasha's mom."

Although Barack lost his 2000 bid to become a U.S. Congressman, he learned a lot about campaigning.

More Change

After Sasha's birth, Michelle began thinking of changing jobs. She interviewed for a position at the University of Chicago Hospitals, taking baby Sasha with her. She made it clear to those interviewing her that her job as a mother was equally as important as any other job. The interviewer was impressed, and Michelle got the job. In the coming years, she would count on her mother Marian and friends to help her juggle a full-time job and family.

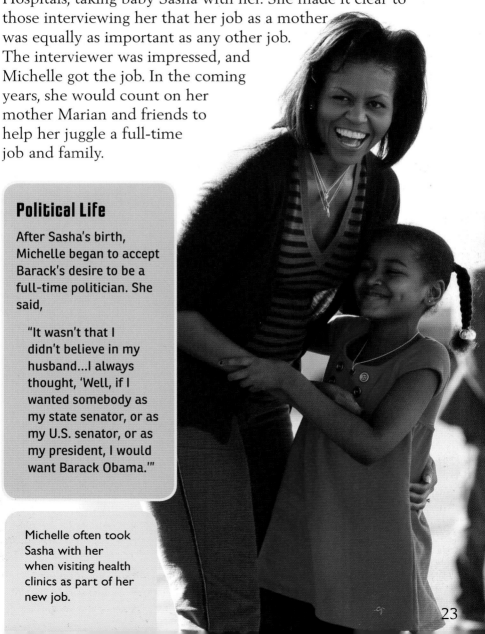

Political Life

After Sasha's birth, Michelle began to accept Barack's desire to be a full-time politician. She said,

"It wasn't that I didn't believe in my husband...I always thought, 'Well, if I wanted somebody as my state senator, or as my U.S. senator, or as my president, I would want Barack Obama.'"

Michelle often took Sasha with her when visiting health clinics as part of her new job.

Campaigning for Barack

In early 2004 Barack Obama campaigned to become a U.S. Senator from Illinois. Michelle was right behind him. She campaigned for him by making phone calls, giving interviews, and stepping in at public events when Barack couldn't be there.

Obama in the Spotlight

In the midst of the campaign, Barack gave a speech that would change the Obamas' lives. In July 2004 he spoke at the Democratic National Convention (DNC) to help presidential candidate John Kerry. Kerry was running against George W. Bush. Before he took the stage, Michelle joked with him. "Just don't screw it up, buddy," she said. He didn't, and the inspiring speech earned Barack a standing ovation and national acclaim.

The Obama home in Hyde Park was called the Western White House after he became president.

Many Americans were introduced to Barack and Michelle for the first time at the 2004 DNC in Boston, Massachusetts.

Mr. Obama Goes to Washington

In November Barack won a landslide victory in his Senate race. Afterward, the family made the difficult decision for Michelle and the girls to remain in Chicago while Barack moved to Washington, D.C. Barack came home on weekends and during Senate breaks. Michelle continued working full time. In 2005 she was promoted to Vice President of Community Affairs at the University of Chicago Hospitals.

Hope and Change

Barack's 2004 convention speech focused on hope and change. He said,

"I believe we can provide jobs for the jobless, homes to the homeless, and reclaim young people in cities across America from violence and despair. I believe that...we can make the right choices and meet the challenges that face us."

A Presidential Election

In 2006 Barack told Michelle that he wanted to be the next U.S. president. He also told her that he wouldn't run without her approval. At first, Michelle was against it. She had told interviewers that she sometimes felt like a single mom. She knew that being the leader of the nation would take even more time away from Barack's role as husband and dad.

The Obamas announced Barack's presidential campaign at the Old State Capital in Springfield, Illinois. Abraham Lincoln served here as state representative.

A Key Role

Wives often play a key role in the presidential elections. During the 1812 election, Dolley Madison's popularity as a hostess may have secured her husband's victory. One hundred years later, Florence Harding managed her husband's public image by approving speeches, setting up photo opportunities, and cooking homemade waffles for reporters.

Florence Harding was the first woman able to vote for her husband in a presidential election.

Making a Decision

Michelle also knew that Barack was the best person to guide the nation in the coming years. So she agreed and threw her support behind her husband. She cut back her hours at work and asked her mother to help with child care. In the coming months, she would be Barack's rock, his biggest supporter.

Michelle had one final condition before she would agree. First, Barack must agree to quit smoking. Michelle had tried for years—without success—to get Barack to quit. And the girls had a demand of their own: whether he won or lost, they would get a dog.

Helping Barack Win

At first, Michelle had difficulty adjusting to life on the campaign trail. Her words and even her facial expressions were carefully analyzed by reporters. Her clothing choices became news stories. And Michelle's sense of humor sometimes got her into trouble. When she said that Barack snored and had bad breath in the morning, for example, some people were upset.

Getting to Know Michelle

As Barack's popularity soared, many of his supporters worried about Michelle. But Michelle's friends and admirers understood that once Americans got to know the future first lady, they would love her. Michelle's intelligence, warmth, and strength could be an important asset to Barack. As a working mother, Michelle also had a lot in common with many American women.

A friendly fist bump between Michelle and Barack received media attention across the nation.

Michelle appealed to women voters by appearing on TV shows like "Ellen."

Michelle made sure to show her softer, caring side. She began appearing in magazines and on television shows that had largely female audiences. She learned to think before she spoke her mind. Michelle quickly became an important asset on the campaign trail. She helped Americans relate to her "intellectual" husband.

BREAKING BOUNDARIES

SOCIAL MEDIA

Barack's 2008 presidential campaign was the first to successfully use social media sites. Campaign officials took to Facebook, Twitter, and other sites to win hearts, minds, and money for their candidate. The Internet campaign allowed Barack to target young voters who were eager to hear his message of hope.

A Historic Election

On November 4, 2008, Americans went to the polls to choose the 44th president of the United States. By the end of the day, it was clear: Barack Obama had become the nation's first African-American president. As the results were announced, the Obama family celebrated at a Chicago rally.

Moving to a New Home

Over the next few months, Michelle focused on preparing for the move from Chicago to Washington, D.C. Her goal was to make the move as smooth as possible for Malia and Sasha. Everything was changing for the girls: they were getting a new home, new school, and new friends—not to mention round-the-clock security.

The Obamas celebrated together in Chicago after Barack's historic election.

Michelle earned high marks for her choice of dress—as well as her poise and grace—at the Inaugural Ball on January 20, 2009.

Preparing for the Big Day

On January 19, the day before the inauguration, Michelle, Malia, and Sasha spent the day at a football stadium. They helped thousands of volunteers put together 85,000 care packages to send to U.S. troops overseas. Later in the day, Michelle hosted an event called "Kids' Inaugural: We Are the Future." Michelle asked kids to get involved by volunteering for good causes.

THEN and NOW

Inauguration Day

Beginning with George Washington, presidents were sworn into office on March 4. This allowed time for votes to be counted and results delivered by messengers on horseback. With the invention of the telegraph, telephone, and automobile, this wait became unnecessary. In 1937 Franklin Roosevelt was the first president to be inaugurated on January 20.

First Lady

After her husband took office, many people wondered what Michelle's role would be. Would she be an activist like Eleanor Roosevelt or Hillary Clinton, and try to influence her husband's policies? Or would she follow the example of first ladies like Barbara or Laura Bush and choose nonpolitical causes to focus on?

Michelle says that Bo, the first dog, is part of the family.

BREAKING BOUNDARIES

FIRST DOG

In April 2009 the newest member of the Obama family moved into the White House. Bo is the first Portuguese Water Dog to live in the White House. He was given to the Obamas by the late Senator Edward Kennedy. The first lady walks Bo in the morning.

Michelle makes sure that her daughters' activities are a top priority.

Mom-in-Chief

Michelle quickly let Americans know that her most important role was Mom-in-Chief. She said, "I wake up every morning, first of all, making sure that my kids get to school on time and they do their homework." Whenever possible, all of the Obamas eat an early dinner together. The first lady often chooses to stay at home with the girls instead of traveling with the president. When Michelle is gone, the girls' grandmother takes on child care duties. Marian Robinson lives in the White House with the Obamas.

THEN and NOW

Sidwell Friends School
Malia and Sasha attend Sidwell Friends School, located in Washington, D.C., and Bethesda, Maryland. This well-respected, private school was founded in 1883. Vice President Joe Biden's grandchildren also go to the school.

Choosing a Cause

After a year as first lady, Michelle introduced the Let's Move! program. The program was designed to fight childhood obesity and promote healthy food and lifestyle choices. Through Let's Move!, the first lady has encouraged schools across the nation to change their menus to include more fruits and vegetables. And she has asked American kids to be more active.

White House Garden

Part of Michelle's efforts to promote healthy eating included planting an organic garden on White House grounds. She grows everything from corn, beans, and squash to tomatoes and strawberries. There's even a beehive nearby for honey. In 2012 the first lady published a book about gardening and healthy eating.

The first lady believes that eating healthy foods and exercising is important for all kids.

Joining Forces has helped thousands of veterans train for and find jobs after leaving the military.

Joining Forces

Another important program that the first lady championed was Joining Forces. The program was created by Michelle and Dr. Jill Biden, the wife of Vice President Joe Biden. The goal of Joining Forces is to help military spouses and veterans find jobs. The program connects 2,000 U.S. companies with military families for training and employment.

THEN and NOW

White House Gardens

- The first White House garden was planted in 1800 by Abigail Adams, wife of second president John Adams.
- In 1943 Eleanor Roosevelt, wife of Franklin Roosevelt, planted a Victory Garden to encourage Americans to grow their own food during World War II.

First Lady, First Hostess

One of the most important roles for any first lady is to serve as hostess for official White House functions. These events can include lunches, dinners, fancy balls, and holiday events. World leaders, politicians, rock stars, athletes, and other famous people have visited the Obamas at the White House.

The Easter Egg Roll has been a White House tradition since 1878, when Rutherford B. Hayes was president.

White House Fun

Some of Michelle's favorite functions include kids. In the spring, Michelle leads the White House Easter Egg Roll. She has left her own healthy mark on this traditional event. Kids can now try yoga classes and participate in food demonstrations. In the winter, Michelle and the girls take part in lighting the White House Christmas tree.

BREAKING BOUNDARIES

DINNER FOR KIDS

In 2012 Michelle Obama hosted the very first Kids' State Dinner. The 54 kids who attended were all winners in the Healthy Lunchtime Contest that the first lady sponsored.

THEN and NOW

Glamorous First Ladies

From the earliest first ladies to today, the presidents' wives attract attention by wearing the latest styles. Dolley Madison shocked Washington by wearing a turban. Grace Coolidge was the first to show her bare arms wearing a sleeveless flapper dress.

Jacqueline Kennedy was one of the most stylish first ladies in U.S. history.

Stylish First Lady

Michelle has also attracted attention for her unique sense of style. She has made headlines in designer clothes, but she also purchases off-the-rack clothing in places like Target, Gap, and J.Crew. Her affordable selections appeal to the average American woman.

Ambassador of Hope

Anytime the first lady appears in public, she is representing the United States. As the wife of the president, Michelle Obama is an ambassador of hope and goodwill. Some of her earliest visits were to schools and homeless shelters in Washington, D.C. Since 2009 she has visited hundreds of schools, military bases, and hospitals across the United States.

International Trips

Michelle Obama's first international trip as first lady was in the spring of 2009. She visited England, Germany, France, and the Czech Republic. Later in the year, she visited Russia to tour schools and hospitals in Moscow.

Not all of the first lady's visits are planned in advance. In April 2010 the first lady made a surprise stop in Haiti. The trip came just three months after the country was hit by a deadly earthquake. She visited a children's center and toured neighborhoods that had been damaged.

Michelle traveled to South Africa with her daughters and her mother.

No Hugs Allowed

When the first lady briefly hugged Queen Elizabeth II, she broke a centuries-old tradition of not touching the monarch. A spokesman for the queen later called the hug,

> "A mutual and spontaneous display of affection and appreciation."

After the meeting, the queen asked the first lady to keep in touch.

Not all of the first lady's visits are with the president. Michelle visited Mexico and Africa without Barack. Michelle, Malia, Sasha, and Marian Robinson met Nelson Mandela. Mandela is a former president of South Africa, as well as a famous civil rights activist.

At the Democratic National Convention, Michelle reminded voters that Barack was still the best person to guide the nation.

Battle for Another Term

In April 2011 Barack Obama announced that he would run for a second term as U.S. president. Once again Michelle was right behind him. This time the first lady's role would be more important than ever. In 2012 polls showed that she was the most popular first lady in decades. Even as the president's popularity declined, Michelle remained loved and respected by Americans.

Democratic National Convention

In September 2012 democrats gathered in Charlotte, North Carolina, to nominate Barack Obama as their candidate. As the convention opened, people anxiously waited for the first lady to take the stage. Many Americans felt that the president had not kept his promises of hope and change. Could Michelle make voters remember why they had supported him in 2008?

The First Lady's Speech

The first lady's speech was a success. As the president and his daughters watched from the White House, Michelle delivered a positive, upbeat message to Americans. She reminded them that Barack was one of them—that he cared about them. In the weeks that followed, Michelle traveled the nation, shaking hands, hugging, and listening to voters. When Americans took to the polls in November, Barack won with 53 percent of the total vote.

Perfect Speech

Michelle Obama's speech was a hit with the media. Anderson Cooper, a CNN reporter, said he had

"never heard such a well delivered speech by a first lady ever."

On the night of the 2012 election, the Obama family again celebrated a victory in Chicago.

What's Next for Michelle Obama?

What's in store for Michelle Obama as she continues a second term as first lady? Before the election in 2012, Michelle said that she would add women's health issues to her causes. She plans to continue the Joining Forces program, and she promised to continue her commitment to fighting childhood obesity. Most importantly, of course, Michelle will continue to be Mom-in-Chief.

No matter what the future holds, family will remain a priority for Michelle Obama.

THEN and NOW

After the White House

When a first lady leaves the White House, there are opportunities waiting.

- Laura Bush wrote a memoir and served as an honorary ambassador to the United Nations.
- Hillary Clinton was elected senator from the state of New York, ran for president in 2008, and served as secretary of state.
- Barbara Bush campaigned for her son, George W. Bush, when he ran for president.

What will happen when Michelle is no longer the first lady? Some have guessed that she will run for elected office. However, the first lady herself has admitted that she doesn't enjoy politics. Many people think Michelle will write her memoir, joining her husband as a published author. No doubt, she would have some fascinating stories to tell.

To Be Continued…

Michelle has called herself a work in progress. Will she return to a professional career at the University of Chicago Hospitals? Or will she focus on community service and nonprofit work? The world will be watching to see what path she takes. No matter what Michelle Obama chooses for her future, there is no doubt she will do it with grace.

Glossary

advocate someone who publicly supports and works for a cause

ambassador someone who represents another person, group, or cause

ancestor person from whom someone is descended

candidate person who runs for elected office

civil rights rights of liberty and freedom guaranteed to all U.S. citizens

commissioner official who is in charge of a department

corporate relating to the world of business and industry

dean person in charge of a department at a university or college

Democratic National Convention (DNC) meeting held every four years to choose the Democratic Party's candidate for president

discrimination treating someone unfairly because of that person's race, sex, or other trait

first lady wife of the president of the United States

homemaker person whose job is to manage the home and needs of the family members

honeymoon vacation taken by a newly married couple

Inaugural Ball party held to celebrate the inauguration of a new president

inauguration ceremony at which the new president is sworn in to office

internship program that gives practical experience to a student in a chosen field

landslide overwhelming victory

memoir story of a person's life, usually an autobiography

mentor someone who helps and guides another person

multiple sclerosis (MS) serious disease that affects the brain and spinal cord

National Mall open area in downtown Washington, D.C., that stretches from the Capitol Building to the Lincoln Memorial

nonprofit company that was not formed to make money

obesity condition of having too much body fat

off-the-rack available at a store; not a designer item

postgraduate program of education that continues after a student graduates from college

prejudice unreasonable dislike of someone or something

priority something that is given attention before other things

recruit convince someone to join a cause or group

social justice making sure that all people in a society are treated fairly and equally

social media sites that allow people to interact with one another on the Internet

telegraph device used for sending messages via electrical signals

yoga system of physical exercises for gaining bodily strength

Timeline

1964   Michelle Robinson is born on January 17 in Chicago, Illinois.

1981   Michelle graduates second in her class from Whitney Young High School.

1985   Michelle graduates with honors from Princeton University in New Jersey.

1988   Michelle earns a law degree at Harvard Law School in Massachusetts.

1989   At Sidley and Austin, Michelle mentors a law student named Barack Obama.

1991   Fraser Robinson dies on March 6.

1991   Michelle takes a job in Chicago Mayor Richard Daley's office.

1992   Michelle marries Barack Obama on October 3.

1993   Michelle takes a job with Public Allies, a nonprofit group.

1996   Michelle takes a job with the University of Chicago.

1997   Barack begins his first of eight years as an Illinois state senator.

1998   Malia Ann Obama is born.

2001   Natasha "Sasha" Obama is born.

2002   Michelle takes a job at the University of Chicago Hospitals.

2004   In July Barack speaks at the Democratic National Convention. In November he is elected U.S. senator from Illinois.

2008   In August Michelle speaks at the DNC. On November 4 Barack wins the election.

2009   In January Barack is inaugurated as the 44th U.S. president.

2009   In April Michelle takes her first international trip as first lady.

2010   Let's Move! is launched in January. In April Michelle visits Haiti, then flies to Mexico for her first solo international visit.

2011   In April First Lady Michelle Obama and Dr. Jill Biden announce Joining Forces, a program to help military families.

2012   The first lady publishes a book about gardening and healthy eating.

2012   Michelle helps Barack campaign for a second term as president.

2013   Michelle attends Barack's second inauguration on January 21.

Find Out More

Books

Besel, Jennifer M. *Malia and Sasha Obama*. Mankato, Minn.: Capstone Press, 2011.

Gourley, Robbin. *First Garden: The White House Garden and How It Grew*. New York: Clarion Books, 2011.

Obama, Barack. *Of Thee I Sing: A Letter to My Daughters*. New York: Alfred A. Knopf, 2010.

Pastan, Amy. *First Ladies*. New York: DK, 2009.

Websites

animal.discovery.com/the-spot/bo-obama/
Enjoy Bo's website on Animal Planet.

firstladies.org
Visit the website of the National First Ladies' Library.

letsmove.gov/sites/letsmove.gov/files/pdfs/healthy-lunch-challenge-cookbook.pdf
Download the cookbook with the 54 winning recipes from the 2012 Healthy Lunchtime contest.**whitehouse.gov/joiningforces**
Find information on Joining Forces at the White House website.

whitehouse.gov/about/inside-white-house/interactive-tour
Visit this site for an interactive tour of the White House.

DVDs

ABC News. *A Moment in History: The Inauguration of Barack Obama*. DVD. MPI Home Video, 2009.

HBO Documentary Films. *By the People: The Election of Barack Obama*. DVD. Sony Pictures Home Entertainment, 2010.

Inside the Obama White House: Brian Williams Reports. DVD. NBC News, 2009.

Index